30 Reasons Why Men Deserve Nothing Copy

Imani Forester

Contents

Terms

High-Value woman: a woman who is confident, independent, and has high self-worth. She has values, boundaries, and expectations, and she prioritizes them in her life, making decisions that align with them.

She is often happy and successful in what she does, whether that be her personal pursuits, education, career - or all three. A high-value woman knows her worth and her value. She understands the importance of a "soft life," free of stress and burden, and so she takes care of her physical health, mental health and overall self-care.

In relationships, a high-value woman is selective, unashamedly so. She sets high standards for the people she allows into her life. Her partner must not only have money, but he must be a kind, generous, and protective provider. She values mutual respect, trust, and communication in her relationships and is unwilling to settle for anything less. She is comfortable being single and does not rely on a relationship for her happiness or fulfillment.

High-Value Man: A man who is not only successful in his career or personal pursuits, but has a strong sense of purpose and direction in life. He is confident without being cocky. He has high self-worth and he is kind, without being a pushover. He has high-emotional intelligence, allowing him to handle challenging situations gracefully and with composure. He cares for his physical, mental, and emotional health and prioritizes self-improvement.

In relationships, a high-value man values mutual respect, trust, and communication and is unwilling to settle for less. He understands, respects, values and actually likes women as people. And he is not intimidated by women, so he feels no desire to compete with them. He is socially apt, likable and engaging. Thus, he feels no need to employ PUA or manosphere tactics to get women. He understands his role as a protector and provider to his woman. He does not expect a woman to "build" with him or go "50/50." He treats his partner with kindness, affection, and support and is committed to building a strong, healthy, happy relationship. He is the true definition of masculinity and strength. Dusties have tried to co-oped the meaning, but any man can have money while still not being high-value. A high-value man must meet all the criteria listed above. A dusty with cash is just a high-earning dusty. High-value men and high-earning dusties are not the same.

A Dusty: this is a male who is often lazy, unproductive, or unmotivated. He isn't actively pursuing his goals or taking care of his responsibilities. Many dusties seek to use women for their own gain, extracting anything they find valuable about her without providing her with anything of value in return. They will use women for anything from sex to shelter, money to a car, food to gifts, to intangible resources like her time, knowledge, education, connections, her ability to build him up, etc.

A dusty often feels entitled to his choice of women, his "dream girls" or "preferences," no matter how far below their league he may be. And he will grow resentful of all women when they do not give him the time of day. Dusty men tend to be obsessed with "getting laid," while simultaneously shaming women for their "body count." They shame women for having standards while also shaming them for "not choosing better."

They criticize the women who seek provider men, while also criticizing the women who further their educations and pursue careers to become financially independent. They are incapable of forming real connections with women, and hardly view them as humans let alone equals. (If you listen to them long enough, you'll hear them refer to human males as "men" and human women as "females." "Female" what? Horses? Goats? They are casual with their disrespect) Because of their inability to emotionally connect to women, women become interchangeable, which is why it is so easy for them to mistreat, use and discard women. Women are merely ego boosts for their constantly diminishing self-esteem.

At the same time, dusties are fiercely competitive with women. They uphold toxic femininity by picking apart women's appearances, right down to their hair, makeup, and nail choices, like bitter and insecure school girls. And will constantly accuse women of being "masculine." Meanwhile, their effeminate nature drives their need to be "the prize" in relationships. Oftentimes, the dusties who grow jealous and resentful of women, coupled with their social ineptitude, will find themselves in Red Pill subsections of the "manosphere," where downtrodden men share toxic, misogynistic, and harmful ideals about women, "gender roles", PUA (Pick Up Artist) tactics, etc.

What most dusties have in common is their deprioritization of a true connection with women, of marriage, family, self-development, and of their role in relationships with women as loving partners who care, provide, and protect.

Pickme Chick / Pickme: a woman who is unable to see the true nature of most men. She believes the rhetoric that men are "biologically designed to spread their seed; thus, they cannot be monogamous." So she tolerates it whenever her man breaks her trust. She is the very definition of a "ride or die," and she believes in "pouring into men" and "building them up."

Overall, she goes out of her way to please men and gain their approval in the hopes of being chosen or validated by them - she does this often to her own detriment. She tends to be incredibly naive about relationships as she is so blinded by love and "can't help how she feels" about her man. She may believe in "twin flames" and justify a poor relationship with a man that way. A pickme's lack of boundaries, values and expectations towards men is why she is willing to regularly compromise her own happiness and needs. All of this reflects her low self-worth and lack of self-respect.

She may excuse and accept mistreatment by men because she desires to be seen as agreeable or as dusties say, "feminine, fit, and friendly." She is willing to "hold a man down" by splitting bills with her, or covering them entirely, allowing men to move into her home, cosigning on his loans, etc. Essentially she is willing to pay to be in a relationship with a man. Yet, despite her generosity, a pickme chick is likely to find herself in consecutive toxic relationships, where the men in her life constantly use her and discard her. Still, she prefers an unfulfilling relationship to the alternative: being single. Pickme chicks will align themselves with dusties in shaming high-value women for wanting softer lives, for their desire to dress up, their self-care practices, and for having high standards for the men they choose to enter into relationships with.

Builder chick: An upwardly mobile woman who may not be a full-out "pickme," but she still tends to date below her standards. She believes love is enough to make a relationship with a man work, and thinks her personal financial success can turn a bum into a businessman. She'll date a dusty for his aesthetics, personality, their "connection," or his "potential," and then invest heavily into him hoping he becomes the business partner she's always dreamed of. She wants to be a "Power Couple" with a man unwilling to empower himself enough to level up his own life. She doesn't accept that you can't teach a man to have drive and ambition. She will end up being used for her resources, and often falls into the *Starter Wife Club*.

High-earning dusty: Essentially just a dusty with money, but they think they're high-value men. They have all the same personality flaws as a regular dusty save, perhaps, for their ambition and drive. However, instead of allowing their low self-esteem to make them lackadaisical, they become driven to "prove" themselves to the world, especially to the women they never had access to before. Some will marry their dream girls when they have the money to afford them, while others will mistreat their dream girls intentionally as a sort of "revenge" for being ignored in the past. High-earning dusties tend to be the ones who will sleep around and become "playboys" well into their 40s and 50s, before scrambling to settle down as old age and health issues set in. At this point, they seek a long-term relationship with a woman so she can be their nursemaid.

High-earning dusties may build their wealth on their own through their career or entrepreneurial endeavors. Still, many will use the labor, finances, and resources of a builder chick, or pickme to help them advance financially. Of course, they tend to abandon this woman once she fulfills her purpose in building him.

FOREWORD

Love can't pay the bills, and money don't cheat – Anonymous

·♥·•·♥·•·♥·•·♥·•·♥·

*W*ant to Be a "Traditional Woman?" Marry For Money.

Believe it or not, the concept of marrying for love is actually quite new, having emerged within the last few centuries. In fact, the love one had for a partner was not why marriage was designed. Originally, the concept of marriage for practical, tangible things like social status and financial stability is an ancient one that dates back to at least the Middle Ages.

During this time, marriages were often arranged by families for strategic and particular reasons, like gaining or maintaining wealth, acquiring land, or political power. That is not to say that compatibility and love were completely absent from these arranged marriages, but romantic feelings were certainly not considered the primary reasons to marry someone. Even as far back as Ancient Egypt, Greece[1] , and Rome, marriages were arranged in order to maintain or obtain wealth or power, or else to "keep bloodlines pure." So, while marrying someone due to romantic feelings towards them may be the most common reason people say their vows today, the idea of marrying for money and social status has been around for thousands of years. Why did it last so long? Simply put, because it worked.

The aim of this book is not to convince women to forgo things like compatibility, connection and love when looking for a long-term partner, but rather to give her permission - should she need it - to seek higher quality men for romantic partnerships. Too many women date and marry for love, only to end up alone, traumatized, impoverished, and sometimes even a single mother after the fact. This goes to show that it is simply not enough to settle with a man based on something as fickle and fleeting as love.

To live their best lives, women must aim to become high-value and seek their proper counterparts - high-value men. Too many women are settling for a dusty because they "love him" or because they see his "potential," and they end up worse off for it.

1. Wolff, H.J. (2017). Marriage Law and Family Organization in Ancient Athens: A Study on the Interrelation of Public and Private Law in the Greek City. Cambridge University Press. Retrieved from https://www.cambridge.org/core/journals/traditio/article/abs/marri age-law-and-family-organization-in-ancient-athens-a-study-on-the-in terrelation-of-public-and-private-law-in-the-greek-city/0B1D402153 1FE79C17F68A6068681794

Chapter 1

Reason #1: If You Build Him, He Will Leave

"When I didn't have any money, I resigned myself to dating women I did not like." - A real-life dusty.

U nlike women, who often marry for love, men who use women - dusties - tend to take what they can get. This type of male will marry a woman whom he does not necessarily love, but who proves useful to him. Let's say a woman is very domestic, and he likes how she cares for the home, he will stay with her for that reason. Perhaps she brings in the majority of the income, he will stay for that reason as well. If he is a more ambitious dusty who dreams of having wealth, and he meets a pickme chick who is ambitious as well, he will often marry her if given a chance. Not because he loves her, but because he is in no financial position to do better.

This type of man is happy to build with a woman. He's often the type that wants to go 50/50 with the person he dates and marries, and wants to know what a woman is "bringing to the table" so that he can know how best to use her. See, unlike most women, most men compartmentalize women, and the importance women serve to them. A hardworking woman who wants to "build together" is a very valuable asset because she helps him get to the next level in his own life. If you become financially successful together, these men are more likely to cheat, or to leave you altogether, as they seek out their dream girl. Every man has a dream girl - the type of woman he would date if money was not a problem for him. And when you help a man to build himself financially, you give him the chance to find her.

When he presents himself to his dream girl as a prosperous man, she may misconstrue him for a high-value man because he has money. She has no knowledge of his immoral and shallow values, nor does she understand how he mistreated the girlfriend or wife who helped him reach his privileged status. All the dream girl sees is a successful man whom she assumes made it all on his own, because she does not see the work that *you* put in. And, of course, he would never tell her.

When he leaves you for the dream girl, he often marries her. Thus, she becomes the second wife who is able to relax and enjoy the fruits of *your* labor and the man you thought was yours. You are left behind as the thankless builder chick ex-girlfriend or starter wife.

Chapter 2

Reason #2: No Man Values Pickme Chicks

Men of all kinds understand that if they desire something badly enough, they must put the work in to obtain it. Whether this is a certain lifestyle, a car, a house, clothes, a watch, or a relationship with their ideal partner - their dream girl. They understand that anything that is valuable must be earned through work, and they view women this very same way.

If you are willing to put up with a man at his lowest, if you are willing to just "love him anyway" as he struggles to figure himself out and make something of himself, he will be grateful to you in the moment. But as he levels up himself financially and mentally, he will look at you differently. He will view you as something that was easy to obtain, that did not require work. Therefore, your value decreases in his eyes, as he realizes he never had to work nor prove himself to you in order to get you. When a man wants something bad enough, he will work hard to get it, and he will work hard to maintain it.

Pickme chicks who "hold down" their dusty men and become their "ride or die" partners are often shocked to be blatantly told by these men that they have "lost respect" for her. Some of these men have even asked them, "as a woman, why would you want a man in my position?" In other words, a man who achieves his goals while you allow him to nest up under you will eventually stand on his own two feet and look back at you with contempt.

"But why? What has happened? What has changed? Why did he switch up?" you may wonder. Well, I'll tell you. Your newly "leveled up" man now sees you as a part of the past that he has transcended, a part of the struggle life he has leveled up from. That is why men almost always leave the women who built them up behind. You remind him of the struggle, you represent his lowest point, and now that he is "somebody," his new partner must reflect his new reality.

"I lost respect for you. As a woman, why would you want a man in my position?" - A real-life dusty after his girlfriend stayed with him during his lowest point in life.

Chapter 3

Reason #3: Providing For a Man is "Masculine."

"Women should be feminine, fit and friendly." – dusties

When you go 50/50 with a man, you will not be rewarded for it. Rather, you will be accused of being "masculine" because dusty men say that the definition of a "feminine woman" is a woman who is a homemaker and takes care of her children and partner. If you are "going 50/50" with a man, working a job to pay bills with him and provide for his lifestyle, by definition, you are in a "provider role" - a man's role. Therefore, you are performing masculinity. If you want to be seen as "feminine" in their eyes, then it is important not to step into their gender role as providers.

Of course, the irony in all of this is that dusties are codependent by nature and need your labor, resources and income in order to survive. They claim to desire "traditionally feminine women" while they are unable to play the role of "traditionally masculine men" and care for their partner, home, and any children they may have together. They may desire the "traditional" housewife of the 1960s and 70s, but they fail to create a secure and abundant atmosphere that would enable a woman to do so.

They desire a "traditional woman" in terms of her servitude and docile behavior alone, but make no mistake; they still expect her to work a 40+ hour job each week, and juggle that with household chores, child-rearing, and taking care of their every desire as well.

Chapter 4

Reason #4: Honor Your Divine Feminine Nature

Everyone possesses the energies of the masculine and feminine within themselves. This is literally the Law of Gender. Feminine energy is the ability to create and to destroy. True feminine energy is also wild. It is intuitive, and it is even chaotic - as represented by Goddess figures of the ancient past like Goddess Kali and Goddess Lilith who portrayed the wild, unrestrained nature of the Divine Feminine. It is also a nurturing energy, but not to just anyone! Unlike how a woman's "nurturing nature" has been weaponized by society to force women into positions where they are submitting and slaving away to men, the Divine Feminine's nurturing nature was originally towards her children. The Divine Feminine is also represented by the action, or rather inaction, of rest, and also of receptivity.

Whereas the Divine Masculine has always been attributed to action and to movement! The energy of the Divine Masculine is commonly understood to be a dynamic, assertive, and purposeful force that drives action and achievement. The energy of the Divine Masculine is often associated with traits like strength, courage, and determination, and it is linked to the pursuit of goals, the ability to take action, and the drive to make things happen.

Of course, men and women benefit greatly from being able to properly yield these two energies that exist within themselves. These are often the people we see realize their dreams, and manifest their greatest desires in life! Ex. An entrepreneur who has a brilliant idea - uses their feminine energy to tap into their creativity - and then takes action and builds a successful business - using their masculine energy to tap into their drive and take action. Also the artist, who taps into their feminine energy and embraces their creativity, nurturing it until they are very skilled, who then taps into their masculine energy by going out and distributing their art wherever they can. They network with people until they're well known, eventually growing a fanbase of people, who are willing to pay them handsomely for their work.

However, in our modern times, where people have been socially engineered, even shamed out of their divine natures, we are left with men and women who have both forgotten the benefits of their divine energies. So that interactions with the opposite sex feel strained, awkward, unpleasant, and unnatural. Men expect women to provide for them, build with them, and will shame women into nurturing and taking care of them like second mothers. And women will ignore their receptive natures, thanks to narratives that tell women not to be "lazy" or become gold-diggers." Hence, women rarely step into their Divine Feminine energy, and instead live in their Divine Masculine, embracing lives of hard work and providing for men who demand they "go 50/50."

This results in women who break down physically, mentally and spiritually, because they've allowed men to use up their energy, their vitality. They age faster. They experience things like chronic inflammation. They experience more diseases and a higher mortality rate due to the stress of working hard physically at jobs, caring for everyone but themselves, and not having the proper food, rest or time to recharge their bodies and minds. Their bodies and energies are out of balance with their Divine Feminine nature that asks that they also sit back and rest, sit back and receive in their lives.

Chapter 5

Reason #5: Gratitude is NOT a Natural Trait of Men, But of Women

·❤·❤·❤·❤·❤·

Reason #5 piggybacks off of reason #4, which states that it is within your Divine Feminine nature to be a receiver and to rest. In this capitalist patriarchy we live in, women have been encouraged to be providers, and to hustle alongside men for money. This hustle culture that women have been forced to compete in, was given a new look, and name, so they would embrace it more - you may be familiar with terms like "Girl boss" and "Boss babe."

Now, there is nothing at all wrong with being your own boss. In fact, I embrace women having their own money, and possessing the freedom to work for themselves - this is a part of living your best life.

But, I also recognize that women are in the best place mentally and physically to be creative enough to start their own business or succeed at their present job, when they feel safe, rested, and relaxed. When we experience chronic stress, the prefrontal cortex (PFC), which is the key area of the brain responsible for executive functions like planning, problem-solving, decision-making, and also creativity - can become impaired, making it more difficult to generate and implement creative ideas. That said, settling for a dusty often results in more struggle, and more episodes of stress in life, which can make it difficult to generate new, effective ideas for any career you may have or for your own business.

It isn't impossible to excel while under pressure, but there's a reason why women who are financially secure and well-rested are able to easily produce creative and lucrative ideas. It is because they live in a state of peace and calm. They don't have to work to survive; they choose to work. Therefore, they are free to work on projects that they are truly passionate about and find fulfilling. These projects become successful, because it isn't desperation or stress driving these women forward, but inspiration, excitement, and often the desire to help others.

When you choose to go 50/50 with a man, or worse, you take care of him entirely, you are not operating in your natural feminine energy of receptivity. Instead, you are stuck in your masculine energy, where you are providing and giving.

If you want to honor your receptive nature, then it is important that you are regularly receiving. Women are naturally wonderful and gracious receivers because they are simply more grateful people. Even small gestures like flowers, a good coffee in the morning, a nice dinner at a restaurant, handling some of her usual tasks for her, a good wine, a romantic date, a thoughtful gesture, are things that make women incredibly happy. Women possess the capacity to show and express incredible happiness and gratitude. Why? Because, they are natural receivers.

Men, on the other hand, are not natural receivers, at least not in general. A woman could receive gifts her entire life from a generous partner and her gratitude would continue to grow over the years. Whereas a man could be in the exact same position as her, and his gratitude towards his partner would eventually shift to resentment, until he became bitter and pulled away from his partner completely. Why? Because, deep down, he knows it is in his nature to provide. So if he cannot meet his basic nature as a man, he'll feel humiliated and get angry, then will project his anger towards his partner.

A few years ago, a video went viral online of a well-off woman gifting her man a rental property for his birthday. His friends watched as he opened his gift, and when they saw it, one exclaimed, "Now, that's a real boss chick right there!" The energy in the video changed at once, and it was clear her man felt embarrassed by her grand gesture. She thought she'd turned him into a property owner, and he could accumulate wealth this way, but his mind was stuck on his friend's words about his "boss chick" girlfriend. The video ends with him trying to recover from the shame by embarrassing his generous, builder chick girlfriend, telling her he would have preferred "a Rolex, a chain..." instead.

His response shocked women all over the net, especially black women, so much that Youtubers made videos about it and women wrote think pieces about it. Most women concluded that such a gift should be reserved for a husband, not a boyfriend, like the man in the video. But they missed the real issue with this situation. You see, as a woman, anytime you are extremely generous and giving to men, you risk making them feel ashamed of themselves. This shame often morphs into resentment, competitiveness, and jealousy towards you! (The man in the video never once thanks his girlfriend for the gift.) You may have the purest of intentions when you pay a man's bills, buy him expensive things, build him up, etc. but men feel like they should be able to provide these things for you, or at least for themselves. They know deep inside that building themselves is their job, not yours. The man in the video felt like his girlfriend had "shown him up" in front of his friends and all over the internet. Hence, his ungrateful, careless reaction.

As much as modern men demand that women "bring something to the table," and go 50/50, in reality, that is not what their nature truly desires. Men are hardwired to feel emasculated whenever they are financially dependent on a woman, especially if she is their romantic partner. High-value men enjoy impressing women with their wealth, and achievements. This makes them feel valuable and useful. And when you are too generous towards a man, you are basically telling him that not only does he have no value, but that you don't need him, and in fact, he needs you. That is a harsh message to send, even unintentionally. If your love language is giving, and you feel you must give to a man, then gestures like cooking a meal he loves is fine, and sometimes small, inexpensive gifts work well too, things like cufflinks or a hat he's been eyeing. Not rental properties as birthday gifts, not covering his meals at restaurants, and not paying half his bills in the home!

It is a real masculine man's desire to be a productive, and protective provider. Of course, rest and relaxation are important for him as well. But it's not nearly as important as his innate desire to give, which makes him feel wanted and fulfilled. A woman who provides for her man becomes masculine in his eyes, and she gives him no incentive to provide for her. In order to feel good about themselves again, some men will be driven to cheating on their provider girlfriends or wives. Often with women who are worse off than them in some way, like a single mother with multiple children, a poor woman, or a less attractive woman, just so they can feel more accomplished than her. This often destroys the self-esteem of his partner, who wonders why he chose the woman he cheated on her with. Some emasculated men may even become abusive towards their partner, because a man without power and control outside his home becomes a danger to his family.

More recently, women have posted videos online going out to restaurants with men they are dating, where they pull out their credit card to see how he will react. The high-value men in the videos will look at their partner with confusion bordering on annoyance and demand she put it away because it is his job to pay. One man even said, "Please, don't embarrass me," in response to his girlfriend's attempt to cover their restaurant bill.

Why the hostile responses to a woman's generosity? Because high-value men get their confidence and self-worth from being self-sufficient, self-made, and being able to care for their loved ones. They gain their pride from the accomplishments they reach on their own or with other men. This is why when men come into money, they are more than happy to find their dream girl and spoil her. They'd never dare demand she split bills with him. Being able to take care of his woman makes a high-value man feel confident, useful and powerful. This is the whole reason why sugar daddies became such a popular concept as well. So, it is important for both men and women's overall well-being that they embrace their natures.

Of course, this is only generally speaking. Men who are providers can also be abusive or cheat. And not every man who is assisted financially by a woman will become ungrateful or resentful. But, it would be foolish to deny that overworked women building with men, or taking care of them financially, don't suffer more spiritually, mentally and health-wise than their well-rested, stress-free, high-value women counterparts who have chosen to partner with high-value men.

Dusties don't want a "boss babe" any more than they want a "gold-digging" high-value woman. Don't get it twisted, they will accept when you spoil them and shower them with gifts like they are the prize, but they will complain about how you emasculated them afterward. So stop paying attention to what dusty men claim to want. They don't know what they want and are incapable of treating you well, regardless.

As well, they don't know or understand all they have to be grateful for. Men are given nearly every advantage in society. They are more likely to be respected when they enter a room, for instance. They are more likely to be taken seriously and be seen as more credible when it comes to any topic. They are more likely to receive business loans and support when starting a business. Yet, dusty males will still complain about the few instances when women are centered – ex. certain events, policies or charities created to center women. Dusty males are so entitled and delusional about everything they are given that they'd complain about "Women's History Month" while ignoring the fact the other 11 months are dedicated to them by omission. They could receive an entire pie, yet would complain about how oppressed they are if women get the crumbs, because having everything is so normal and expected for them. *This* is the danger of being overly generous to men, they grow blind to all they have been given, and become incapable of appreciating it.

And, if you are trying to "build" a dusty man in your life, in hopes that you can change him into the high-value man of your dreams, well, you can't turn a bum into a King. If you are seeking a man of high value, then only date those who took the initiative to better themselves in your absence, those who built themselves before they ever encountered you. Remember, men have the privilege in this society. Therefore, you should be able to build yourself off of him. He should be helping you get ahead in life. Your connection to a man should have tangible benefits for you.

Chapter 6

Reason #6: You Gain Upward Socioeconomic Mobility When You Don't Settle

As stated earlier, in the past, unions like marriage were made in order to maintain wealth within families. Or to pass wealth to families and individuals. Oftentimes, the transfer of wealth would be from a man to a woman, and their future family together.

Unfortunately, things have not changed too much. Studies have shown that most women in the top 1% earners of America got there through marriage. Yes, despite the huge percentage of women who are attending post-secondary schools, and becoming entrepreneurs, the economic glass ceiling is so thick that women are still not scoring the highest positions in companies in order to be paid more.

And, when they go out to start their own businesses, which is a very wise move, they face gender-based prejudice. If they are women of color, then they face both race and gender-based prejudice. What this means is that they are less likely to get funding for their businesses, and their businesses are more likely to fail, than men's businesses on average. Hence why most women in the top 1% of Americans economically, married into it. Only five percent of elite households include women who have earned enough money to qualify for 1 percent status, according to a recent study [1] in the American Sociological Review. This gender disparity has remained consistent for more than two decades. Instead of relying on high-paying employment or extensive education, a woman's best chance at entering the top 1 percent is marrying someone with "strong income prospects." On the other hand, men's best chances of reaching the top 1% of society is through career and academic successes.

As well, out of all of these marriages, only 15% of them relied on the woman's income in order to achieve that 1% status, meaning the majority of men in the top 1% of Americans were able to obtain their wealth on their own. They didn't need a woman to build with them or go 50/50.

---

1. Newburger, E. (2019, February 22). A woman's best route to the top 1 percent is to marry rich, research shows. CNBC. Retrieved from https://www.cnbc.com/2019/02/21/a-womans-best-route-to -the-top-1-percent-is-to-marry-rich.html

I did not give you this information to convince you to try to marry a top 1% earning man. Rather, I gave it to you so that you can keep in mind that studies have shown that whoever a woman marries is one of the main factors contributing to her future economic status. Who she settles with will determine if she, and any future children she may have, will live a life of financial ease or a life of struggle and poverty.

There are financial consequences for women who choose the wrong man and then leave him as well. In fact, numerous studies have revealed that women suffer more financially than men after divorce or separation. On the flip side, males tend to experience greater financial success in the aftermath of a breakup.

A study by sociologist Richard R. Peterson[2] revealed that a woman's income and quality of life decreased by 20% after a divorce, along with an almost 30% heightened risk of poverty. Whereas men typically experienced a 30% increase in their income and quality of life after separation.

This is why it is imperative that you do not settle for just any man. This warning is especially pertinent for black women, who often find themselves bearing a disproportionate amount of the financial responsibilities for their households; in fact, 80% of black mothers are either the sole breadwinners or make up at least 40% of their household's total income. When they choose to settle for dusty partners who are financially less successful than themselves, not only does their household's overall wealth fall, but their personal wealth falls as well. It is due to this that black women face an extremely high risk of poverty at a rate of 62%, compared to even black men who face a risk of poverty at 50%. This discrepancy is never talked about in mainstream media, but Black women need to be especially careful

---

2. Peterson, R.R. (1989). Women, Work, and Divorce. SUNY Press.

about who they choose to partner with in order to protect their financial futures and overall quality of life. Feeling sorry for their counterparts while ignoring their own plight is literally counter-productive.

All women must take it upon themselves to seek out relationships, which offer stability. That means doing the research and due diligence necessary to determine if a potential partner is financially responsible, has a clear plan for their life, and most importantly, values them as an equal. Once a woman has found her ideal partner for the long term, she needs to have open and honest conversations about money management, investments, and other financial topics in order to ensure that everyone remains on the same page going forward.

Chapter 7

Reason #7: Your Health Depends On His Wealth

Health is like money, we never have a true idea of its value until we lose it."—
Josh Billings

There are numerous advantages to having an elevated socioeconomic standing. More often than not, this reflects positively on a woman's quality of life and health. By dating someone within or superior to her financial standing, a high-value woman will be able to access fresher food sources, reside in regions with fewer pollutants, and have access to better medical care should she ever need it.

A high-value woman dating a high-value man can also be relieved of everyday burdens like household chores like cooking and cleaning, because her man will be in a financial position to hire assistance so his partner is not overwhelmed with housework. Furthermore, when women are more careful with the kind of men they choose to partner with and have children with, it is more likely for her man to be able to provide luxuries such as daycare, caregivers or sitters, which can help to alleviate even more stressful tasks that would usually fall on women in relationships.

This, of course, results in a woman who is healthier than her pickme chick counterpart, who chose to settle for a dusty and who lives a life of more financial struggle. Women who settle for dusties often deal with more financial hardships, and are burdened with more duties within their relationships, so they are more likely to be chronically stressed as a result. It's been well documented that chronic stress causes inflammation and leads to disease.

Our health is our most important form of wealth. If we do not have our health, we have nothing. A wealthy, terminally ill person would trade it all to be well, and often do. And so, our health is something that we must take seriously, and make decisions that are going to help to increase and prolong our health in this lifetime.

Even if you manage to build with a dusty, and eventually reach a higher socioeconomic position together, the amount of energy, and stress on the body required to do that will have taken a huge toll on your health long-term. It is wiser to choose a high-value man who does not need your money, nor your labor, to survive.

Chapter 8

Reason #8: Your Happiness Is Impacted By Your Income

One says that money doesn't buy happiness. Without a doubt, one was speaking of the money of others – Sacha Guitry

Women cannot afford to settle for dusty men because settling for a man who needs your income in order to survive, actually causes increased unhappiness in life. While it's been conditioned within us to believe that money doesn't buy happiness, many people understand that the relationship between happiness and money is much more complex than that. Here's the truth: indeed, money does buy happiness. We see that through better health outcomes of wealthier people alone.

In 2016, a study conducted by researchers at Purdue University aimed to measure happiness and its relationship to income globally, in order to find out the ideal income required for individuals to maximize their emotional well-being and life satisfaction. Here is what they discovered, in order to be emotionally well in 2016, an individual needed to make between $60,000 to $75,000 each year, which in 2023 is approximately $75,456.80 to $94,321.00.

To live a satisfying life, Purdue University[1]'s study discovered that an individual's ideal income needed to be between $95k - $105k each year, which in 2023 is between $119,473.27 to $132,049.40 per year. Obviously, it should be noted that the more affluent the area you live in, the higher your salary often needs to be for you to feel happy and emotionally well. The researchers found that people who earned less than this threshold tended to experience more stress and worry, while those who earned more did not experience a significant increase in happiness.

But, what is particularly troubling about these numbers, is that consumer purchasing power has decreased thanks to inflation, so no one's money is going as far as it used to, adding to unhappiness. Also, the aforementioned figures don't pertain to an entire family, or even a couple. These income numbers are for one individual alone. This is why high-value women cannot afford to settle for dusty men who want to use them financially. A woman today would need to be earning at least $150,913.60 in

---

1. Purdue University. (2018, February 13). Money only
   buys happiness for a certain amount. Retrieved
   from https://purdue.edu/newsroom/releases/2018/Q1/money-onl
   y-buys-happiness-for-a-certain-amount.html

order to make enough money to achieve optimal happiness for herself and her man, and at least $238,946.54 for their collective life satisfaction.

Chapter 9

Reason #9: Dusties Make Poor Life Partners (Literally and Figuratively)

Being dusty is not simply a number in a man's bank account. A man in his late 20s and beyond, who is still broke, who is using women for resources, whether they are women he is dating, or his mother, often have personality traits that are unbecoming.

Being dusty is a series of personality traits as well as a mindset. A dusty man often possesses personality traits like laziness, lack of ambition and drive, and a scarcity mindset. He is more likely to be a negative person who often complains about how "unfair" life has been to him. As well, he is often aimless and unsure of his calling in life.

Overall, this kind of man is struggling to take care of himself. Therefore, how can he take care of you? How can he take care of children if you choose to have them together? Instead of dating, it is in the best interest of these kinds of men to focus on self-development. Develop a more positive mindset, heal emotional trauma, money blocks, and hone skills and talents that they can use to increase their incomes and improve their lives.

You don't want to settle for a partner who is codependent on you and unhealed in every way, who has no idea where he is going in life and cannot take care of himself, nor you. Successful relationships tend to occur between people who are on the same page, and going in the same direction. Therefore, high-value women work best in relationships where they and their partner share similar, positive and healthy mindsets.

Chapter 10

Reason #10: Providing and Protecting are Baseline Requirements

Women who truly know their worth never entertain broke, or dusty men. These kinds of men tend to be stingy, mean, or manipulative so they can take from you. Why? Because they don't have enough on their own. When you refuse to settle for this caliber of men and date generous, provider men instead, high-value men, you see an immediate shift in the treatment you receive.

High-value men tend to be more generous and thoughtful, because they enjoy helping and feeling needed. It is important to note that not all men with money are high-value men. There are plenty of mean, stingy and manipulative men with money - high-earning dusties. High-value men not only have money, but they are generous with it. They enjoy the act of giving without expectations, it's not tit for tat with them.

In contrast, some dusty men may try to masquerade as high-value men upon first meeting them, but they will quickly show their true colors. For example, the man who will take you on a dinner date and generously pay for your meal, but in exchange for the dinner he expects that you will have sex with him. And if you don't, his true, angry and entitled self will emerge as he throws a tantrum. These are the kinds of dusty men who often refer to themselves as "nice guys." High-value men are not like this. They are satisfied just knowing that they can make you happy, that they can be of assistance to a woman they like, and they don't "act nice" in hopes that you will sleep with them. They are content with a simple smile and a "thank you." It truly makes their day and is a fulfilling act for them because they are caring people. High-value men are wealthy of bank account, mind, and spirit.

There are dusty men online everyday complaining about high-value women's standards and expectations. If you ever stumble across their videos or podcasts, you may quickly notice that the only time that these dusties want to talk about love, is when women bring up money. It isn't genuine of course. It's just an attempt to make women with standards feel shallow.

They *know* love can't pay the bills. They're just hoping *you* don't.

Chapter 11

Reason #11: Dusties are Walking Red Flags

"It's just as easy to love a rich man as it is to love a poor man." - Anonymous

Most dusties are in the position that they're in because they have not made an effort to become anything more or change their circumstances. If a dusty was willing to put in some effort, he could drastically turn his life around. Therefore, 9 times out of 10, if you come across a dusty man, he is not putting effort into bettering himself and his life overall. And if he is unwilling to put effort into fixing his own life, he will be even less likely to put effort into making a relationship work with you. He is also less likely to put effort into building a life with you, and raising any children you may have together.

This is often how so many women end up single mothers, or "married single moms" where they are doing everything - paying the bills, caring for house and home, caring for both their children and their dusty - all while feeling utterly abandoned by their dusty man in return. As for the dusty, he will lay up and do nothing, just like he did when you first met him.

You may wonder why dusty men are like this. Well, it is because men prefer the path of least resistance. If a man can get what he seeks with the least amount of work possible, then that is what he will choose to do.

If you give a man your time and attention, you provide for him, you take care of his child, give him sex whenever he wants it, do all the housework, and he doesn't need to lift a finger, then guess what will happen? He will never bother lifting that finger ever again.

Dusty men are red flags. *Just run, sis.*

Chapter 12

Reason #12: Settling Makes Finding a Good Man Hard For All Women

Women already do so much in relationships. Many give men the "wifey" treatment, where they will literally act like a doting wife towards a man they are dating, only for him to never marry her. Yet, because of the manosphere rhetoric and "gender war" agenda being perpetuated all over the internet these days, dusty men have convinced themselves, and they are trying to convince you, that *they* are the prize. Even though they chase women, they still ask women what they have to offer. They want to be taken out, they want flowers and money. As ASAP Rocky once famously said, "women should take him shopping," because he's "handsome" and "a bad bitch." And unfortunately, he is not alone. Men everywhere are beginning to feel this way too.

When pickmes gas up dusties, and make them feel like being subpar is more than good enough, despite the fact that all they do is use women, when pickmes reward dusties for doing absolutely nothing but existing, when dusties realize that there is no need to become better people, when they realize there is no need because women are going to spoil them regardless, it lowers the quality of available men in general.

If you let them, most men will sit back in their feminine energy and receive from you, using you until you are tired and worn out from having to be in your masculine energy for your entire relationship. Then they will complain about your lack of effort in your appearance, your lack of energy, your lack of interest in them, and they will tell you that you have changed and that you are bitter. When in reality, they were the catalyst for this change. When in reality, you're simply just tired, and they don't possess the emotional intelligence to even see that.

Chapter 13

Reason #13: It Affords You the Luxury of Free Time

The Greatest Luxury is Being Free - Manolo Blahnik

Women who find themselves in a situation with 'dusties', are usually putting in double the effort: half for her and half for him. They are constantly working hard just to keep up their standard of living, with little time left over for self-care. This can lead to physical and mental exhaustion over time.

When you are a high-value woman dating or married to a generous provider, you are able to enjoy the luxury of free time. Your free time can be spent however you decide to spend it -- more travel, self-care, cafes, reading, working out, or however you choose to decompress.

It is in their free time that many people are able to enjoy their hobbies, or learn new skills that can improve their life. Maybe you want to enroll in a class or take a course. All these options can be explored when you have the free time to do so.

Chapter 14

Reason #14: You Can Start a Business and Become Financially Independent

"When a woman is financially independent, she can live life on her own terms."

It's not only pickmes that shy away from dating high-value men. Sometimes high-value women and builder chicks also avoid seeking out high-value men out of fear that she may lose her financial independence. After all, we know that not all men with money are good people. Some are just high-earning dusties who use their money in order to control and abuse women. This book is about teaching you why you shouldn't sell yourself short by settling for a dusty partner, and how high-value men are the better option in all aspects.

But, the idea isn't simply to live off of a high-value man and his generosity. No matter how much money your partner gives you, nor how many of your bills he takes care of for you, you always want to make sure you possess your own nest egg. In fact, your provider man should be giving you money on the regular, like an allowance, that you can use for whatever you please. You see, anything can happen in life that can impact his ability to provide for you. He may become injured, laid off of work, his business may get slow, or you may eventually break up, but if you have been saving and growing your own money the entire time, then you always have a soft place to land.

When you are with a high-value man, you should also take advantage of the fact that you have the time and money to learn about entrepreneurship, investing, and other means of making money. High-value men love being helpful, so you should ask him to fund your financial endeavors, and also ask him to teach you what he knows about finances – whether that is the stock market, business, etc. You should be able to learn from your high-value man, and he will be happy to help.

Don't just spend the money he gives you on material goods that will lose their value. Level up and develop an abundant mindset where you are always seeking opportunities to make money work for you, so you can live a life of financial freedom with or without a man in the future. This is why I strongly suggest starting a business with some of the funds he gives you, something that does not require years in school. Something you can start right away with tons of scalability like: an Etsy business, self-publishing, starting an Amazon FBA or arbitrage business, creating an affiliate blog, a Youtube channel, tutoring online, a Shopify store, a Fiverr business, an eBay store, selling on Facebook Marketplace ... you get the picture. Buy a good course or training program if needed – don't be cheap when it comes to your financial future. Give yourself the best chance to succeed.

The thing about any business is that it can take some time to build and grow, but when you aren't worried about the expenses, you don't have the added pressure of trying to make your business work by a certain date because the bills need to be paid. Instead, you can take your time, and grow your business properly, because you know that your high-value man is taking care of the bills. Similarly, if you decide to invest some of the income he gives you into stocks, you don't have to concern yourself with seeing returns right away because the money you invested is not immediately needed to pay bills. Thus, you can rest easy knowing that you are growing your revenue streams and that if it takes some time to see the full impact, it will not negatively affect your livelihood.

Chapter 15

Reason #15: When You Step Out of Survival Mode, You Can Step into Your True Power

"To live is the rarest thing in the world. Most people exist, that is all." – Oscar Wilde.

It's a sad reality that most people are struggling financially. Of the people living in first-world countries, women in relationships with men, still living paycheck-to-paycheck, are in that position largely because they have chosen to settle with a dusty. Dusty men are inherently codependent. They can hardly manage to take care of themselves, so they often rely on your income in order to survive or to "build." But the result is that they drag down the standard of living of the women they are with. That's why when you date dusty men, it becomes very difficult to leave survival mode.

With a dusty, you're always hustling and trying to figure out how to make the next dollar. When the next bill payment is due, how much debt you owe, and how you can make more money are concerns that are constantly on your mind. You are never able to step into your true nature as a creative being, and thrive!

Despite how much we have been collectively brainwashed, the true nature of human beings is not struggle and survival. It is joy and abundance. A brilliant man named Bob Proctor wrote a book entitled "You Were Born Rich." And it went on to sell millions of copies all over the world. It still sells today, decades after it was published, because truth resonates with people. We were born abundant.

God, the Universe, Mother Nature, whatever you call this great power that created us all, it gave us a world full of abundance. Have you ever seen an apple orchard in the Harvest Season? Left unpicked, the trees bear so many apples that they fall to the ground, covering it like a carpet! The Earth provides more than enough for her children, both human and animal alike. God did not create the concept of scarcity on this Earth - humans did. That is why it is so important to shift out of the survival mode and the scarcity mindset they have conditioned us into.

When you escape "survival mode," you can truly step into your true power and become the person you were meant to be. When we are not stressed about money and work, the human mind is free to focus on things most people never get the chance to. You can think about problems people face in the world, and ideas flow to you on how they can be resolved. Most of the world's problems are very much solvable, but the capitalist system we are forced to live under ensures that most people are too busy scraping by and trying to make ends meet to find the solutions. Did you know that most of the ancient Greek philosophers did not work because they were wealthy and came from rich families? They were some of the only people in their time who could afford to sit around and ponder existence and reality. Everyone else had no time for deep thoughts because they had to get up and work to put food on the table. Think of all the problems in the world that would disappear if more people had time to think about how to solve them? They would be operating from their higher selves instead of their fear-based lower selves. Imagine if we could collectively create and plan humanity's future, instead of merely planning so we can survive until next month? One thing's for sure, our world would look very different.

When we are at rest, we are free to observe the world around us. We are free to think and to create ways to help all of humanity live better. When we move beyond the "survival" state, and into a state of calm, we transform on the spiritual level as well. We discussed how a calm mind increases creativity, but it also improves your natural intuition, your innate abilities, and increases your frequency, too so you can manifest the things you want in life much more easily.

The most beautiful things that humans create are often born when we are in a higher state of mind, when we are thriving energetically, instead of scraping by. If you want to discover your true potential, you need to shift out of your desperate, survival mode energy. And, that is a very difficult thing to do when you are forced to go out and hustle each day because you are responsible for splitting bills with a grown man who claims he is "building with you."

Chapter 16

Reason #16: It's NEVER 50/50

"Marriage is not a flex."

– Women who have awoken to the truth and can't be shamed or gaslit

anymore.

We hear it so much in today's world: Men who claim they are looking for a low-maintenance woman, who is feminine and will "submit" to them, but this woman must also hustle and provide him with half the money for all the expenses in their relationship. Essentially, these men are seeking submissive providers. Like many things dusties claim to want, this concept is contradictory and nonsensical - the sexually experienced virgin woman, anyone? Ugh.

The idea of "going 50/50" sounds logical in theory - both parties should contribute half of the financial expenses in their relationship. But it is a flawed concept because it assumes that men and women bring the exact same amount of energy, time, work and commitment into every other aspect of their relationship as well, when they really don't. "Going 50/50" is impossible in the context of a relationship between men and women and there are studies that can easily prove it. These studies are easy to find, so I'm unsure how or why pickmes and builder chicks fell for the 50/50 hoax, but here we are. The truth is, thanks to gender roles constructed under the patriarchy, women actually put a lot more effort into relationships than most men. Women are the ones often tasked with chores like cooking and cleaning, on top of doing the majority of child-rearing.

In 2018, the United Nations published a study that found that women, globally, perform 2.5 times[1] more unpaid household work and caretaking than men do. Unpaid work refers to tasks that are not compensated like household chores, cooking, cleaning, taking children to appointments, doing the majority of child-rearing, caring for elderly family members, and other domestic tasks. This type of work, though essential for a functioning household and community, is often undervalued and overlooked.

But it gets worse. Studies have shown that women also carry the majority of the emotional labor in relationships. In fact, UN Women chief of research and data Shahra Razavi has said that societies around the world don't see women's work as valuable, but that if women stopped doing all their unpaid work, then "the whole economy would collapse[2]." While people may think this only means calling, texting, and making plans, it also refers to the energy that one puts towards their partner. This includes wor-

---

1. ILO. (2022, September 18). Closing gender pay gaps is more important than ever. Retrieved from United Nations News website: https://news.un.org/en/story/2022/09/1126901

2. Carpenter, J. (2018, February 21). The unpaid work that always falls to women. CNN Money. Retrieved from https://money.cnn.com/2018/02/21/pf/women-unpaid-work/index.html

rying about them, managing their partner's health, initiating important emotion-based conversations, emphasizing with them when they are going through a difficult situation, coming up with thoughtful surprises and gifts, etc. When women take responsibility for the majority of unpaid and emotional labor, the U.S. Department of Labor noted, men had more time in their day for exercising, playing games and other recreational activities. In contrast, all this extra work puts a strain on women, leaving them with less time and energy to relax, engage in their own hobbies and interests, and makes it harder for women to advance in their careers compared to their male counterparts.

A man who wants you to cover 50% of the financial expenses does not intend to also split the household chores, child-rearing, and emotional labor with you. Make no mistake about it. He expects *you* to cover all of that on your own. He just wants you to pick up some of his responsibilities as a man. In reality, when a man says you should go "50/50," what he really means is 80/20. *Run, sis!*

Chapter 17

Reason #17: Because They Told You to "Choose Better"

You shoulda CHOSE better! – All dusties after one of them screws you over

T he phrase "you should have chosen better" is often used by males to criticize or belittle women for their romantic choices. When men use this phrase, they are often suggesting that the woman has settled for someone who is beneath her, and they infer that the woman made a poor decision in selecting a partner.

This kind of criticism can be particularly hurtful, as it suggests that the woman is responsible for the problems in her relationship and that she should have "known better" than to choose the man she did.

However, in reality, the opposite is often true. Many women tend to feel pressured to settle for men who do not meet their standards, due to societal or cultural expectations, or because they believe that they will not find anyone better. This can lead to unhappy and unfulfilling relationships.

Once again, the black community is infamous for this. You know it's bad out there when a 7-figure earning lawyer is shamed all over the internet for not wanting to settle for a bus driver.

Although, women collectively have been shamed at one point or another whenever they express interest in a provider partner. So if you're going to be criticized either way, whether you find a man who meets your standards, or you lower your standards to spare dusty men's feelings, choose yourself and what will make you happy in the long run.

Raise your standards if you haven't already and keep them up. Shamelessly only entertain men who meet your criteria and make you happy. Don't settle for men who can't provide, who don't treat you well or who do not share your values and goals, just to appease dusties. Because, as soon as things go south with these males, it will be other dusties shaming and belittling you, telling you "you shoulda chose better."

So don't wait for them to say it. Listen to me say it instead: Choose better, sis. Choose yourself and your happiness. Find a partner who is a good match for you and who will treat you with the respect and love you deserve.

Chapter 18

Reason #18: Break Generational Curses of Poverty

Modern Slaves Are Not in Chains. They Are in Debt – Anonymous

Because who you choose to settle with is a large, determining factor in whether you will end up financially secure in the future, the person you decide to partner with can actually help you to end generational curses of poverty in your family lineage!

Even if you grew up in poverty, even if your parents grew up struggling financially, and their parents as well, it can all end with you, if you are wise and selective when choosing a spouse. You see, marrying a high-value man helps to level the playing field in societies where systemic economic inequality prevails. When you date and marry with purpose, you are able to raise your offspring in an environment where their needs are easily met.

You and your partner will have the means to create a trust fund for your children.

Also, in this environment, you can comfortably plan and save money for their secondary-school education without issue. So many young adults from lower-class families understand the importance education plays in improving one's financial future, this is why many choose to attend post-secondary schooling. The trouble is, the tuition prices are so high that by the time these young adults graduate with their degree, they are drowning in student loan debt. Meaning they are beginning the rest of their lives far behind their wealthier counterparts.

When you choose a high-value spouse to raise your children with, your children will not have to suffer in the future, struggling under the weight of student loans. Thus, you give them a headstart in life to grow the wealth, you and your spouse have saved up for them, and they can continue to build on it throughout their lives. This is how you successfully end the cycle of poverty in your family.

If you choose to raise children with a dusty man instead, you can be sure that you will have no wealth to pass down to your offspring most of the time. In fact, they may even inherit debt on top of their student loan and other bills. Thus, continuing the generational curse of poverty and struggle in your lineage.

Chapter 19

Reason #19: You Can Live with a Quiet, Calm Mind

When you choose a high-value man over a dusty, you can live with a quiet and calm mind. This is because you aren't burdened with the unnecessary stress brought on by settling for men below your caliber.

High-value men tend to be stable and secure, which immediately reduces the financial stress and anxiety that often plagues women who choose to partner with dusty men. Financial stability alone creates a sense of calm and security, which will reduce tension and conflict within your relationship. This is important to note when you consider that recent studies have listed monetary issues as the third leading cause of divorce in married couples, making up 22% of all divorces.

High-value men tend to have a strong work ethic and are committed to providing for their families. This sense of responsibility also creates a sense of stability and predictability within their relationship, which can lead to a more peaceful and harmonious home environment.

Finally, unlike most dusties, high-value men tend to have a positive attitude toward life and a strong sense of purpose, which can lead to a more optimistic and uplifting home environment. This positive attitude can create a sense of calm and positivity within the relationship, which reduces stress and promotes greater emotional well-being.

So many dusties claim to "want peace" within their relationships. Meanwhile, they are so delusional and out of touch with themselves that they don't even realize *they* are the ones who bring tension and conflict to all their relationships. What's more, they refuse to play their part as caring and communicative men who provide security and financial stability to their partner and children if they have any.

Choose a man who cultivates a peaceful relationship and you will be quiet and calm of mind, at least more often than not.

Chapter 20

Reason #20 – It Doesn't Get Any Better Than This

At the beginning of a romantic relationship, "The honeymoon phase," where you're still getting to know each other, you have not truly met the real man yet. Rather, you have met his representative. Men, like women, tend to be on their best behavior during the early stages of a relationship, doing all they can to make their partner feel valued and loved with romantic and thoughtful gestures. They may try to be extra communicative and attentive to their partner's wants and needs. This helps to build a strong foundation for that relationship. It also helps to establish trust and respect. This is because they want to make a good impression.

Often as men grow more comfortable in a relationship, and as the honeymoon phase fades, the intense emotions of excitement and passion may fade. After the honeymoon phase, many women agree that men change significantly at least three times within a relationship. The first time is when you become exclusive because they no longer feel the need to *try* as hard to keep you. The second time is when you move in together. Sometimes this is because the woman is depending on them to some degree. And the third time is pregnancy, when a woman is physically her most vulnerable. Therefore, she must put a lot more faith and trust in her partner. These changes can be for the better or for the worse.

Of course, the right man will always remain thoughtful, attentive, caring, helpful, protective and will continue to "date" you long after the honeymoon phase has ended - this is what strengthens your connection, and keeps things interesting and romantic. But, considering how many men grow comfortable and stop trying to some extent after a certain point in their relationships with women, you must consider what this means when it comes to a dusty.

If you begin a relationship with a dusty and in the "honeymoon phase" he is already displaying red flags like selfishness, stinginess, laziness and entitlement, what exactly do you think he has in store for you when you become exclusive and he knows you aren't going anywhere? How do you think he will treat you should you ever move in together? Or should you ever become pregnant with his child?

A dusty will not magically morph into a caring, protective provider. Instead, he will reveal even more of his unsavory traits, because he knows that you have chosen him out of all the men in the world and that there's no way he is going to lose you.

Too many women have been brainwashed to think they can "change," "save" or "fix" a man. They think they have the *Midas Touch* that will transform a dusty man into a high-value man. They think that marrying a dusty, or siring his child will make him a better partner, but none of this is true. When you are willing to settle for a dusty man, you are setting the relationship bar on the ground. Understand that the only place that a relationship will go after a dusty no longer feels the need to *try* anymore is to *Hell*. The dusty does not get any better than when you first met him. So if you don't like what you see when you first start dating him, it's time to pack it in.

Chapter 21

Reason #21: A Man Is Only as Good as His Current Status, Not His Potential

Too many women get caught up with what a man claims he wants to do in the future. Whether he wants to be a content creator, an entrepreneur, sports star, a musician or something else, too many women, largely pickme chicks, will stand by and even "build" with a man in whom she sees potential. In theory, it makes sense because, at least he is ambitious, right? He's thinking of his future. He may even be incredibly talented at what he loves, so he'll definitely make it and you can be his cheerleader and reap the benefits of his success later on in life, right?

Well, here's why it's not worth "dating for potential." Firstly, potential is not a guarantee. It's based solely on who your man could be in the future, not who he is right now. There's no guarantee that he will fulfill his potential, even if he has promising traits or qualities.

Secondly, dating for potential often leads women to sacrifice their own dreams and goals, in hopes of helping their dusty achieve theirs. This sometimes looks like taking up a job you hate so you can help pay the bills while your man works on his goals. This can even look like quitting a job you really love, and/or moving out of your city or country so your man can chase his dreams. All these things can lead to an unequal power dynamic in the relationship, as both you and your man are prioritizing his future.

Thirdly, if you are investing in the relationship based on the potential of your man, it can lead to resentment and disappointment if your man does not live up to those expectations. Especially if you have sacrificed so much for him, and put your own dreams and goals on hold or traded your dreams for his. You can easily be left feeling like you've wasted your time.

Finally, the whole time you're building up your man, sacrificing for him, believing in him, he might be thinking, "I can't wait to get where I want to be so I can get the girls who require me to be successful from the very beginning. Those are the high-value women - the 9s and 10s. They know they deserve the best, and I will be able to have them when I'm at my best."

That's right, the whole time that you are dating a man for his potential, he could already be deciding your relationship's expiry date, and plotting to replace you.

It's a little-known fact that most men attach a certain value to the women in their lives. They may prioritize some relationships over others, and many even place expiry dates on their relationships with women. This is something women should be aware of. You might think you're going to spend the rest of your lives together, that it's you and him against the world, and you'll ride or die until he is successful in his endeavors. Meanwhile, your man may lead you on because you are useful to him in the moment, but deep down he knows he has no intention of staying with you. This is what birthed the "starter wives club" and "bitter ex-wife" stereotypes - women being self-sacrificing and overly nice to men because they "love them" and believe in their potential.

This is why dating for potential can lead to settling for less than what you truly want and deserve in a relationship. It's much smarter to focus on what a man brings to the table right now, rather than what he could potentially bring in the future. If he wants you badly enough, he will make something of himself and work to get you. Remember, men do not approach their dream girls empty-handed. They approach them as confident, accomplished people.

Save niceness for your family, your children, other women who are good to you, pets, animals and plants. Men don't like "nice" women. Why do you think men - and boys - trip over themselves when it comes to "bad bitches?" Why do you think women like Megan Fox, Nikki Minaj, Kim K and Charlize Theron have been so desired by men over the years? Men like and respect women who don't take shit from them, women who don't need them but *want* them, women with standards who would *never* accept them based purely on their potential.

They may claim they don't, but the moment men have money, they are chasing down all the "gold-digging" high-value women they can find, spoiling them with lavish gifts and dinners, oh, and marrying them too!

Chapter 22

Reason #22: More Men Are Getting Alimony From Their Exes

When you possess more money as a woman and you choose to settle down with a dusty, or even if you don't earn a lot of money but you are the primary earner in your household, you risk having to pay that man alimony if you separate. Historically, alimony was typically paid by men to their ex-wives after a divorce. This was based on the traditional gender roles where men were the primary breadwinners and women were primarily responsible for domestic duties and child-rearing. However, as women's roles in the workforce and society have evolved, and more men are living off women or being "house husbands," so has the way alimony is awarded.

In recent years, there has been a rise in women being required to pay alimony after splitting with their male partners. In fact, in 2012, a survey of the 1,600 members of the American Academy of Matrimonial Lawyers revealed that nearly half had seen an uptick in the amount of men receiving alimony payments, as reported by Reuters[1].

This is partly due to more women entering the workforce and achieving higher salaries. In cases where the woman earns significantly more than her ex-husband, a judge may determine that she should pay alimony to help support him. Additionally, some states have changed their laws to make alimony more gender-neutral. This means that judges are no longer automatically assuming that the man should be the one paying alimony. Instead, they are considering factors such as each party's earning potential, the length of the marriage, and any prenuptial agreements.

If you are a builder chick, or a pickme who is footing most or all the bills, this should concern you. So many women are going to school, earning degrees, and landing great careers. You can believe it is hard work. Don't allow your hard-earned money to go to waste paying alimony to a dusty ex who you allowed to live on you. Remember, men tend to fare much better financially than women after separation. In comparison, women are more likely to fall below the poverty line. One bad relationship can literally ruin your life. ...Or, at least set you back significantly. This is all the more reason to seek out a partner who earns more money instead of settling for one who earns less than you. Don't give a dusty the chance to make you his next income stream or retirement plan after you break up.

---

1. Williams, G. (2013, December 24). More men get alimony from their ex-wives. Reuters. Retrieved from https://www.reuters.com/article /us-divorce-alimony-men-idUSBRE9BN0AW20131224

Chapter 23

Reason #23: He May Not Like Women, and That's Okay.

Only take advice from someone you'd trade places with. - Jordan Belfort

The dusty men who get the angriest about the concept of having to build, provide and care for a family tend to share one thing in common. They display irrational jealousy, and even complete disdain for women in general. These dusties demand to know *why* they must perform their role as men when seeking a woman, which includes being capable, and protective providers. Many share the sentiment that women don't contribute anything to the world, that they don't deserve anything and that their precious resources are wasted upon women and children.

They get upset at the idea of a woman having a social media account and *gasp* followers who "like" her posts. They get upset about the fact that a high-value man will invite a woman he fancies to a dinner date and pay for it, or invite her on a yacht. These males never compare themselves to high-value men. They never look up to high-value men and gain the inspiration to improve themselves, so they can get the life and the kind of woman they want. They seem angrier at the high-value women who accept kind gestures from generous men. It makes you wonder who dusty men are actually jealous and bitter towards, high-value men, or the women they date? Often, it seems like the *latter*.

It's fine if a man has no natural desire or instinct to care for a woman. But, he should realize it's unusual for heterosexual men to feel no emotional attachment to women. Sure, it's been normalized all over social media to feel disdain towards women and girls, but that's because there is a "gender war" agenda being waged upon both sexes. Men, unbeknownst to themselves, are being "red pilled" by the manosphere to become less and less likeable people, and more entitled and misogynist, so that they are largely unappealing to women. The men at the helm of the manosphere, benefit from their bitter, lonely male followers because they can manipulate these men into purchasing their PUA and loser manifesto books, courses, and workshops.

It must be stated that many people have questioned the sexualities of podcasters in the manosphere, who claim to help men "get women," due to compromising videos and photos of them with other men, that have made their rounds online. One once openly declared that people should advocate for "men who want to be with men." And there aren't enough of these podcasters you can count on a hand who are actually in long-term and healthy relationships with women. Many have been divorced several times, are unmarried and are neglectful fathers if they have any children. Therefore, it is important that men be mindful who they are taking advice from. They say, "Only take advice from someone you are willing to trade places with."

Ultimately, a man who does not like women, hates to see them treated well, and feels competitive towards their achievements, needs to consider the idea that he may not be heterosexual. And, that is all right. In this day and age, plenty of people are loving who they want to love fearlessly and unapologetically. From an early age, boys and girls are socialized to be straight. When two children of the opposite sex are playing together, adults will ask, "is that your little girlfriend?" Or, "is that your little boyfriend." And we are all pushed deeper into accepting a heterosexual identity from there. It's no wonder more and more adults are just now discovering their true feelings about their sexuality. It's also no wonder so many adults are confused or closeted.

That said, if you are a dusty who hates the idea of women getting attention from provider men who care for them, it may be because deep inside *you* desire to be in her position. This may also be why you feel women don't "deserve" anything, or that women "have it so easy." If you are tossing and turning at night, thinking about the wonderful life some men give their women, subconsciously you probably wish you could have the same thing. When women post photos of themselves online and their friends and/or fans tell them they look "amazing, beautiful, stunning, etc." the reason you might hate it so much is because you're comparing yourself to her in your head. You are thinking about how little positive feedback your photos receive in contrast to a woman's, and you wish yours could get the same reaction. You don't want to admit it to yourself, but you are in competition with women.

Countless women have revealed that try as they might, the men they dated or married, were unable to bond with them the way they were able to with "the guys." And it's no surprise considering that many men are *homo-romantic* – only able to form deep, emotional connections with fellow men. Many men are also homosexual.

Hence, men don't have to interrogate women over the value they bring to the table. As well, there is no need to demand a woman prove why she is worthy of being in a man's life. A true high-value man does not *need* a woman for anything tangible in his life. Like many dusties have pointed out, a man can hire a cleaner, a chef, a therapist, and even an escort if he desires. But, a straight, high-value man will choose to have a woman in his life because he actually *enjoys* the company of women. He is capable of forming close bonds with women, and he geniunely appreciates and likes the woman he chooses as a person.

While this book is far too short to go deeper into this subject, complete with studies and resources for males who feel this way, it is certainly something I recommend they do in their free time. It is not some "joke" I am trying to make, but a real possibility that I suggest any man who finds himself jealous of women explore. Men who like women do not feel so hostile towards them. That said, gay men, in general don't feel hostile or jealous of women either. Gay men who embrace and know themselves actually cultivate healthy, loving and wonderful relationships with women, just on a non-romantic level. They have no reason or need to hate on women who get the men who meet their standards, because they are able to get the men who meet their standards too.

At the end of the day, no one is forcing all men to like or want to be with women. If it's not for you, it's not for you. Live your truth.

Chapter 24

Reason #24: Globally Men Are More Employed and Financially Stable Than Women

Men and women will have pay equality in 257 years - World Economic Forum

T ruth doesn't care about dusty tears and bitter feelings. Across the globe men are more employed than women, and they receive higher paying jobs as well. Some male authors have published books that contain blatant inaccuracies about reality in order to push their narrative that men are the oppressed gender and victimized gender in society and that women have lives of wealth and ease due to feminism and "woke" culture. They argue that employers demonstrate bias in favor of feminine applicants over male applicants when granting career progress and new hires. Their dismissal of reality is disconcerting, and the fact that so many men blindly soak up their words without properly researching and verifying the information for themselves speaks to so much of what is wrong with the world today.

Here are the real facts, studies have shown that around the world, women face fewer chances of making money than men.[1] Female participation in the labor force is almost half that of male workers: just over 50%, compared to 80%. Women are less likely to be hired for formal employment with wages and have fewer prospects for advancing their businesses or careers. When women do work, they receive lower compensation than men. Newer research from recent households indicates that the gender gaps have grown more pronounced during the Covid-19 pandemic.

Of course, the wage gap is especially hard on women of color. For instance, Black women need to work 579 days to make what white men do in 365. On average, they are only paid 63 cents for every dollar earned by their non-Hispanic white counterparts. This means a median wage gap of over $2,009 per month and almost a million dollars over the course of a 40-year career. If both a Black American woman and a white American man started

---

1. International Labour Organization (ILO), Organisation for Economic Co-operation and Development (OECD), & World Bank. (2022, January 9). Female labor force participation. Retrieved from https://genderdata.worldbank.org/data-stories/flfp-data-story/

at 20 years old, the woman would have to work until she was 83 just to equal what man made at 60 years old.

[2] LeanIn.org and McKinsey & Company conducted a five-year study, where they observed the presence of women in the corporate world. Between their data from 600 organizations and 250,000 employees, they found that there was an underrepresentation of women in higher-up positions, especially at the senior level. They attributed this discrepancy to what they called *the broken rung* — a phenomenon observed at the beginning of the career ladder when transitioning from entry-level to management. At this crucial point, there is a noticeable difference in the number of men and women chosen for promotions and job positions, with men being greatly preferred. In fact, for every 100 men promoted or hired as managers, only 72 females earned the same position; this resulted in men holding 62% of managerial roles while women held just 38%.

This discrimination at the outset results in a wide difference between men and women throughout the entire career pipeline. Women make up 48% of entry-level staff, yet they account for only 21% of C-suite positions. While males occupy more than half of starting roles, by the time one reaches executive-level, the 78% of these jobs are all taken by men. Over the next five years, this broken rung will result in about a million women stuck at the low rung of the ladder while their male peers ascend.

What could be leading to this extreme gap? *There is clear evidence that gender bias affects who is chosen for promotion and leadership opportunities.* In 2019, just one fifth of executives were female. Studies also suggest that women have to present much greater proof of their capabilities in order

---

2. LeanIn.Org and McKinsey & Company. (2019). Women in the Workplace 2019. Retrieved from https://leanin.org/women-in-the -workplace/2019

to be seen as equal to their male counterparts.. Women are held to higher standards than men and must work harder to demonstrate their worth.

Surprisingly, many workers are unaware of the inequality in their own companies. Despite only one-third of managers being women, an astounding 62% of male workers and 54% of females are convinced that men and women are equally represented in top positions.

Many people also think the situation will improve over the next few years. Over half of HR leaders and employees predicted that gender parity in leadership roles would happen within 10 years. Unfortunately, if current trends continue, it's been expected that it may never happen. As for eliminating the existing disparity in earnings between male and female employees? Experts at the *World Economic Forum*[3] anticipate that men and women will have pay equality in an *absurd* 257 years. The researchers stated that it was unlikely that any of us would witness gender equality during our lifetimes, nor would most of our children.

While these real figures are depressing to all if not most women and girls reading this, understand that I did not write this all to trigger you. Instead, I sought out factual data to point out just how absurd and self-sabotaging it is for women to be financially supporting grown men. This society has made it so that any man is more than capable of supporting himself, and you. Any man who is struggling to make money in these times, does not need to be dating or in a serious relationship with a woman. And any woman who realizes she is dealing with a dusty, who is relying on her income in some form or fashion, needs to let that man go and stop trying to force him into a serious relationship with you. He needs to be financially

---

3. The World Economic Forum. (2020). Global Gender Gap Report 2020. Retrieved from https://www3.weforum.org/docs/WEF_GG GR_2020.pdf

independent when he approaches you, or he will have you working to take care of him for the rest of your life. Who has time for that?

The capitalist system we live under was designed for men to easily acquire more resources than women. Therefore, men should be generously giving to the women in their lives. Women literally cannot afford to do the opposite. *Period.*

Chapter 25

Reason #25: You Were Programmed to Choose Wrong

Messaging from the media has shaped the minds of countless generations, oftentimes for the worst. From promoting smoking as harmless, to pushing dangerous stereotypes, we've allowed the media to think for us and decide what is real.

That said, it's a hard truth to accept but throughout the ages women and girls have been programmed and groomed to pick the wrong men to engage with for relationships. And this poor decision we've been tricked into making starts in our childhood with cute Disney movies and fairy tales, that make us believe in *"true love that lasts forever."* As you get older, it's the charming romantic comedies and the cute Hallmark holiday films that sweep us off our feet and get us dreaming of the perfect romance. But if you notice, all of these stories start with the couple meeting, and end when they finally get together. *Maybe* they'll get to the altar, but then the story abruptly ends. The director never decides to allow the audience a 3-years follow up of couple's marriage or relationship.

Coincidence? No. Strategic. See, a lot of the time, the women in these stories have settled and their lives after the movies have ended – well into a marriage or long-term relationship – would actually be quite undesirable and difficult. It would ruin all the romance the writers worked so hard to create in film! See, the women in these stories always favor "character" over everything, and so they choose a man based on their mutual "love" and nothing else. Usually this means they often end up with the "nice guy" or "funny guy" who brings nothing to the table besides a cute face and jokes. He usually lacks qualities like the ability to protect, self-reliance and financial independence, so he has few resources and ways of providing for a woman or children. But time and time again, he is made to look like the better choice compared to a more responsible, protective, independent high-value man.

These movies paint the female main character as a woman who is mature and pure-hearted, because she isn't "shallow" enough to look down on a man for being broke. At the end of the film, the audience cheers when we see her make the "right decision" by marrying the "nice guy."

The issue is that these kinds of stories make up most, if not all, the narratives young girls (boys) and women are exposed to. This results in young girls internalizing so many harmful stereotypes, like the idea that men with resources can't also be good people capable of providing them with a life of safety and more calm, or that men who have little resources to offer are all sweet and loving people who are above "material things." And that love is enough to sustain a long-term relationship. They show young women that they should lower their standards, because some men are diamonds in the rough whom you should stand by until they become the diamonds they were always meant to be. (*Aladdin*, anyone?)

Movies like *The Princess and The Frog*, taught young girls that the broke, dusty, cute guys who are trying to find a woman to live off, are worth giving a chance. Poor Princess Tiana will probably spend the rest of her days hustling in her restaurant until old age, considering there's no indication that Prince Naveen ever gets his inheritance reinstated after his parents cut him off at the start of the film.

The messages in movies and TV also misguided young men, showing them, "See? It's okay to approach women for serious relationships as long as you're kind-hearted. That is enough. Everything else will work itself out. You will get the girl because you deserve her. And if she has standards, well, it's because she's a stuck-up, gold-digger who deserves nothing." There are rarely any depictions of men taking accountability and bettering themselves to become suitable mates to women in movies. So, boys grow up into men who feel entitled to women without doing any inner work. Then, they grow bitter towards them when women turn them down.

These stories never show young women what a long-term relationship looks like when they settle for a man below their standards, because it is undesirable. It likely looks how most unhappy marriages do: an overworked wife who becomes resentful and bitter towards her husband, because she is forced to work, do all the household duties and care for the children. And a husband who switches up and becomes lazier, more selfish and uncaring towards her.

Because women are not shown the reality of settling for partners who rely on them financially, physically and emotionally, while only contributing to half the bills in exchange, newly married women have NO idea what they are walking into after they say "I do" at the altar. And by the time they figure out how unequal, stressful, lonely and laborious a marriage to a selfish, broke dusty man can be, it is too late. They are locked in with children. Men have even admitted to purposely getting women pregnant as a means of controlling her, so that it is harder to leave him.

It's funny how men gripe about marriage, and how it is a trap set up to ruin their lives. When in actuality, men benefit far more than women within marriages, from longer life-expectancies to lower rates of depression, to having a personal caretaker, chef, cleaner, therapist and caregiver of his children. Oh, and let's not forget that women assist men in growing their wealth during marriages. Studies[1] have shown that when men marry, rather than simply living with a woman, they experience a greater financial gain, known as the "wage premium." On average, this marriage bonus adds about .9 percent to the annual income of men.[2] So it seems that young girls are indoctrinated from an earlier age to lower their standards and desire marriage to men whom they have to "build," "hustle with" or take care of. Perhaps this was done intentionally to ensure that all men in society have a loyal, hard-working woman to take care of them. Meanwhile, the quality of the women's lives are of less concern to society as a whole, hence why married women's life expectancy is lower, and so many are depressed,

---

1. Phillip Cohen, "Cohabitation and the Declining Marriage Premium for Men," Work and Occupations 29, no. 3 (2002): 354.

2. Robert F. Schoeni, "Marital Status and Earnings in Developed Countries," Journal of Population Economics 8, no. 4 (November 1995): 357. All as cited in Patrick F. Fagan, Andrew J. Kidd, and Henry Potrykus, "Marriage and Economic Well-Being: The Economy of the Family Rises or Falls with Marriage," (May 2011). Available at http://marri.us/research/research-papers/marriage-and-economic-w ell-being-the-economy-of-the-family-rises-or-falls-with-marriage/.

overworked, underpaid, and end up facing poverty after divorce, yet this issue is seldom brought up in the mainstream, because women's lives just don't matter as much as men's lives in a patriarchy. As far as the collective is concerned, women were created to slave away and to serve. And if they need to be conditioned, programmed and tricked into this role as little girls, so be it.

I say, forgive yourself not being aware of the game being played on women and girls. But now that you know better, it is important to do better. Don't become just another disappointed and jilted wife in the future. Choose your partner wisely, refuse to be stuck doing all the unpaid labor in a relationship, have expectations that your partner must meet or else it's a deal breaker. And make sure you receive something tangible and useful from every relationship with men in your life, whether that is money, experiences like trips, or actionable advice you can use to grow as a person like business advice, health, etc. And never, ever pay or split bills with him.

You may have been programmed to choose wrong as a child, but every program can be rewritten. It is possible to reprogram your mind for relationship success and satisfaction.

Chapter 26

Reason #26: He May Never Leave ... Even If You Want Him To.

Be careful who you allow prolonged stays at your house. If you start dating a man and the relationship seems to go lightening fast, and next thing you know he's moving in with you, you may have a hobosexual on your hands. Hobosexual is a term used to describe a dusty man who dates women, with the intention of manipulating them into believing they are in a long-term relationship in order to secure a place to stay. The danger with these kinds of men, besides the obvious fact that you don't really know who you are allowing into your home, is that you may not legally be able to kick him out of your house when things eventually go sour. They often prey on young or naive women with little dating experience, who live alone and are just starting out on their own in life, as they will be slow to recognize the hobosexual's bullshit.

See, depending on where you live there are laws that allow house guests to become tenants after a period of time. In the USA, in the state of Texas for instance, if you allow a man to stay in your home and there is evidence that you split bill payments with them, or that he has used your property as his mailing address, this can be enough to suggest to the state that he is an implied tenant (even without a written lease). In these instances, the only way to properly remove him from your home is through an eviction served through court. And that is just a lot of time, energy, stress and money wasted on a situation you wouldn't be in if you knew the law, and weren't so generous to men.

You can protect yourself from all of this hassle and headache by not allowing random men you are dating to live with you. In fact, if you're dating someone and at some point, they imply that they are "between homes" or "between jobs" and they need a place to stay, they may not actually be interested in you but may just be looking for someone who's willing to house them. Kindly decline, and level up your standards.

Chapter 27

Reason #27: Dusty Men Are Cheap With Everything

A cheap man is one who puts a price on everything and a value on nothing. - Winston Churchill

usty men are not just cheap with money. They are cheap with their time, emotions, and effort. They are not willing to do anything that is not "their job." They won't please or nurture their wives and will never "pitch in" to be helpful. They will watch you struggle with tasks before you finally have to ask them for their assistance. Only then will they help you, albeit begrudgingly.

The children of dusties have spoken out about their experience living with them online, and no matter which corner of the Earth they are from, the children of dusties tend to share the same experiences and sentiments. Dusty and broke men make cheap, stingy, and selfish fathers. They won't share with their own children – not money, not resources, and they will not share their love with them either. His family will not feel loved.

Dusty men have nothing to give because they know they have never spent time working on themselves, gaining skills, building wealth, growing emotionally and mentally. Therefore, they know they have nothing of value to offer. They have no material wealth, and they have no wealth of character either. That is why their lack of value shows in their material life and their emotional life too. There's nothing there. So be wary of men who are cheap, broke, and stingy. They are showing you what they have to offer, and here's a hint: it is nothing.

Chapter 28

Reason #28: The Patriarchy Was Designed For Men to Succeed

Women will never be as successful as men because they have no wives to advise them. - Dick Van Dyke

Pickme chicks and dusties will often use the excuse that "things are so difficult for men in this world," that the expectations placed upon them, the pressure to "make it" is unfair to them, that the bare minimum is good enough, and sometimes even less than the bare minimum is completely acceptable depending on the race of the man. Essentially, a man just existing is a grand achievement.

In reality, any man can aspire for more in his life and do well. This might mean getting a degree, but it can also mean learning a trade. Men should not be praised for doing the bare minimum. In the black community for instance, some men have went online and openly stated that women should require less of them, in comparison to other men, because "it's so hard for them." They say that they have to work so hard to get to zero, let alone succeed.

The problem with this mentality, however, is that black women are the most educated group of people[1] in the USA, and they are the largest growing group of entrepreneurs. This is despite the fact that within a patriarchal society, they have their gender working against them, and being a part of a minority group, they have their race working against them too.

Black men only have their race working against them in society. They benefit from being born male. Thus, black men do not have harder lives than black women. Similarly, White men, Asian men, Hispanic men, no group of men collectively have a more difficult time succeeding in society than their women counterparts. If women can survive despite all the setbacks they face in patriarchal societies around the world, men can more than survive, they can thrive in a world designed to benefit them.

Thus, there is no reason that you, as a woman, should feel more sorry for any group of men than you do for yourself, or any group of women and girls in this world. A man "having it hard" because he is male, or because of his race" is just an excuse some men use to explain why they have done nothing with their lives. Do not allow them to gaslight you into settling for them. You are doing something with your life, a man is more than capable of doing the same, and statistically speaking, he is more likely to succeed

---

1. National Center for Education Statistics. (2018-2019). Degrees conferred by race/ethnicity and sex. Fast Facts. Retrieved from https://nces.ed.gov/fastfacts/display.asp?id=72

based on his gender alone. Yet, still, each day, courageous, ambitious, strong women go out and chase their dreams, and achieve them. Men can do this too. If a dusty has gotten nowhere in life while living in a world crafted for men's success, then at some point, that is his choice.

Chapter 29

Reason #29: Men Are the Real Gold-diggers

In our present society, women are born with value. Whereas, men must build their value. Men will whine in manosphere spaces about this, as if women decided things should go this way. When in reality, it was their beloved patriarchy that decided men are born without value and must create it. Women did not create this system, they were merely born into it.

That said, men become gold-diggers in order to create their value in this society. This is especially true for men who come from a lower socioeconomic class, who did not inherit an empire from their fathers. They will seek out a woman who is willing to help them build that empire. During this time, men will put aside their desire to form a relationship with their preferences, their dream girls, and settle for a woman who is willing to build with them. These men understand that pickmes and builder chicks bring financial value to their lives in the present moment, so that later on when they are "made-men," they can go after who they truly want.

This is why it tends to be the broke, dusty men who get so angry at upwardly mobile women for having standards for their romantic partners, particularly when those women desire a man who is of equal wealth or who earns more than themselves. Dusty men understand that the fewer women available who are willing to stick it out, sacrifice and build with them, the higher the chance that they will be forced to put on their big boy pants, and build their wealth and value all on their own.

Women are constantly shamed into lowering their standards, or else they are "gold diggers," while simultaneously being criticized for not "choosing better." (Black women get this more than any other group of women even though they tend to settle the most) A woman can be a young and successful six-figure earner with their own business, and wear a dress size 4, and spiteful, parasitic dusties will still call her "average at best," and demand she settles for one of them. They essentially want her to become a second mother, a builder chick, providing for a dusty and investing in his future until he has enough wealth and value to leave her.

It's a disgusting and sad practice that only continues the poverty among certain groups, since a woman's wealth is often depleted during and after these relationships - especially if the dusty leaves her with a child.

If you desire to date and marry with your partner's money in mind, dusties, and their pickme chick counterparts, will demand that you focus on a man's character instead. They will never say the quiet part out loud, but I will. And here it is: dusty men can't practice hypergamy with you if *you* are practicing it too, sis.

The way they see it, there can only be one sugar baby in a relationship, and a dusty will fight you for that position.

Chapter 30

Reason #30: Men Must Build Value and Even BUGS Know This!

It is natural for the males of a species to pursue the females of that species, and not only that, but they know better than to bring nothing to the table. This has been witnessed by researchers and scientists all throughout nature. In the wild, as males compete with each other in order to secure a female mate, they have developed ways to built their value so that a female will choose them. Males achieve this with anything from displays of their impressive appearance, to providing provisions, protection and care.

Some male birds attempt to attract a mate by showing off their appearance, skill and hard work. For instance, male peacocks have elaborate, colorful tail feathers that they spread out in order to attract females. Male wrens will go as far as building numerous nests in hopes that a female will be pleased with at least one of them and choose them as her partner. Bowerbirds are known as little architects because they craft wondrous homes made of grass, complete with an immaculate front garden that they sweep with a twig, and decorate with flowers and pebbles, as gifts to potential female counterparts. This is how some bird species show that they are capable of building and providing for a mate and any offspring they may have in the future. Male beavers build dams and lodges to create safe and stable homes for their families. Male seahorses carry and incubate their offspring in special pouches, demonstrating their ability to provide for their young. Male lions defend their pride against rival males and predators to protect their females and offspring.

In the bug world, the males demonstrate even more intense gestures of generosity and self-sacrifice. Male brown widow spiders will often put themselves in harm's way as a form of sacrifice to the females they are trying to mate with. During copulation, he will place his abdomen close enough to the female's fangs so that she can consume him after mating as nourishment for their offspring. Redback spider males take things one step further, and will do a somersault right into their partner's mouth after mating. This display is fatal yet beneficial, as males who are willing to make such a sacrifice have twice as many offspring as those who don't. To avoid the danger of being devoured by their mates, some male species have become quite resourceful. Male nursery web spiders, for example, have developed a tactic to increase their chances of survival: they show up with food offerings - insects - for their female partner, as part of the courtship ritual. Researchers [1] found that males who arrive bearing gifts, *are far less likely* to be cannibalized than those who come empty-handed.

Even bugs understand that the female is the prize! Male bugs recognize the importance of bringing something of value to any potential mate. Male spiders will either present the female with gifts, or if he *brings nothing to the table* he will place *himself* on the table, because he cares for the female's health and wants to ensure that she has the nutrients she needs to bear healthy offspring. A male bug has the sense to understand that they both benefit from his sacrifice. So when human males complain about having to build their value, they know they are not acting within their male nature. And the females of different species display their choosiness when it comes to partners by only coupling with the male who shows he can take care of her and a family. There is no "feminine, fit and friendly" in nature. Females don't "settle" because they feel sorry for a male who cannot build or provide for her. She will simply not entertain him, she might even kill him if he is weak because it is disrespectful. Fortunately, humans don't live by insect politics.

When dusty men try to shame you for having standards, please understand that they are asking you to go against your very nature as a female. They claim that men are driven by their inherent desire and their hormones to procreate with "as many females as possible," but why aren't they also driven by the male desire to build and provide for female mates as observed all throughout nature? Could it be that they are picking and choosing which *instincts* they follow? *(Hint: men already know what they need to do. Some are just lazy, and shouldn't be rewarded for it.)*

---

1. Scharping, N. (2021, June 21). Sexual Cannibalism: Why Females Sometimes Eat Their Mates After Sex. Discover Magazine. Retrieved from https://www.discovermagazine.com/planet-earth/sexual-cann ibalism-why-females-sometimes-eat-their-mates-after-sex

It is natural for males to pursue females, and for females to select the most beneficial one for herself and potential family. This can be viewed at the cellular level in humans: the sperm swims towards the egg. The egg does not need to swim towards the sperm. And it goes further than that, it is *the egg* that makes the final choice as to which sperm will fertilize it. That's right, women choose the best partner for themselves even at the cellular level! This has been proven thanks to a study conducted by researchers in Sweden and the U.K. They found that even though the fastest sperm will reach the egg first, the egg makes the final decision in which one will fertilize it. You can research the study called, *Chemical Signals From Eggs Facilitate Cryptic Female Choice in Humans.*[2]

In societies, when tragedies would occur, there would always be a call to save the "women and children first." This was understood and accepted by all because women tend to be a child's primary caregiver, they tend to be a child's first teacher. They are capable of repopulating a group should most people be wiped out, and women are the keepers of culture. These are just a few of the reasons why our society sees inherent value in women, even if it has strict conditions like age, etc. This is not to say that I agree with all of it, personally. I only mention it to remind you that this is the system that MEN built. Men decided that while women had inherent value, theirs must be built. Why dusty men complain to women about their own system and beliefs is just evidence of their desire to be victims.

Regardless, knowing your value in this society as a woman, you should find it unacceptable for a man to approach you with the intent of dating

---

2. (Fitzpatrick, J.L., Willis, C., Devigili, A., Young, A., Carroll, M., Hunter, H.R., & Brison, D.R. (2020). Chemical signals from eggs facilitate cryptic female choice in humans. Published in the Proceedings of the Royal Society B, 287(1929), 20200805. DOI: 10.1098/rspb.2 020.0805.)

you, to then ask you, "What do you bring to the table?" Realize that he is merely trying to belittle your existence, reinforce harmful gender stereotypes, and create a power imbalance where you are petitioning for his approval of you. These dusty men believe *themselves* to be the prize, and they want to know whether *you* believe this as well.

When a man approaches you, understand that he has already acknowledged your value prior to speaking to you. Why else would he approach you in the first place? Whether consciously or subconsciously, he knows that YOU are the prize. Therefore, to answer the question of "what you bring to his table" is to cheapen yourself. Dusties only ask women this question to determine what kind of woman she is: a high-value woman or a pickme chick. And please notice that men never pose this question to women they truly want.

A man will never approach his dream girl and ask her what she brings to the table. Her value is in her appearance, her attention, how she makes him feel and her time. That alone is good enough for him, and he will happily invest his time, money and attention into her. She isn't required to know how to cook or clean. She needn't have a degree nor a high-paying job, etc. (Think of all the male celebrities who have dated and married regular, everyday women)

A man asking a woman to convince him of her value is being disingenuous and rude, and he is aware of this. He knows there's a risk you will lose interest in him and walk away, yet he still asks. Therefore, if he is willing to lose you over a petty and rude question, he is just not that into you.

Always walk with your head held high, knowing that YOU are the prize, and don't entertain dusties and their mind games. Find a man who not only recognizes your worth, but treats you like a valuable person whom he wants in his life. You can't go wrong.

Chapter 31

What If I Can't Find a High-Value Man? I Don't Want to "Die Alone."

This is a common scenario thrown in the face of any woman who dares to have standards. Dusties will tell you "there aren't enough high-value men to go around. And the available ones would never choose you. Good luck dying alone with three cats."

They tell single, childfree women (and women who have children but are single and looking for a decent man) this as an attempt to threaten them, and frighten them into choosing "any man" over facing the possibility of having no man.

What they fail to realize, or perhaps they just don't want *you* to realize, is that studies have shown that the happiest women are actually, single and childfree women. As well, studies show that they live longer than their married counterparts on average. Why? Because relationships are so physically and emotionally taxing and women shoulder the majority of the labor that goes into them. Therefore, they are most stress-free and relaxed on their own. These dusties are basically threatening you with a good time while hoping you won't realize it, and will instead jump into an unfulfilling relationship with them so they can suck you dry of your resources, and leave you when they've drained you of your vitality, time and money.

Living with three cats, plus Mr. Peace and Mrs. Quiet sounds FAR more appealing. Besides, single women have more time to put into their interests, their job, and their pets or plants. And as for relationships outside of a romantic partner, women are more community-minded by nature. A single woman is more likely to reach out to her friends, and spend time bonding with her family members, nieces and nephews as well. Research has shown that women are more likely than men to participate in group activities and community service where they can meet new people while giving back to the public.

Whereas major studies and news articles have been published all over the internet citing the rise of single, lonely men. This phenomenon is a growing issue because single, lonely men tend to suffer from greater mental health issues like depression, compared to their married male counterparts. Single men also have a lower life expectancy than their married counterparts.

There is no doubt in my mind that the manosphere podcasts circulating every social media platform available, coupled with the gender war agenda, are contributing to single, lonely men, incels, and dusties who believe they are the "prize" that women should pursue.

The truth is, any man who tells you that your standards will be the reason you "die alone" is merely projecting his own fears for his life onto you, and hoping you fall for it. High-value women and pickmes differ in their idea of men and relationships. While a pickme chick is just happy to be chosen for a relationship by any man, no matter the quality, and will happily settle just to say she is "taken" or "married," a high-value woman has standards that men must meet. She will not back down or compromise on them, and she has no problem being single until or unless she finds the man that is suitable for her. She knows that a bad relationship is far worse than being single. No woman ever looked back on her dating life and thought, "damn, I should have lowered my standards." Instead, women often look back and wish they had raised their standards.

High-value women tend to find who they are looking for because they operate from an abundance mindset. They understand that dating is a numbers game and the more people you meet, the higher your chances of meeting the right guy. They date rotationally so they don't waste their precious time on the wrong guy – unlike how most women were taught to date just one man for years. The purpose of rotational dating, dating a few men at once, is so you can directly compare them. How does each one treat you? How much effort do they put into your relationship? How do you feel with them? (Loved? Safe? Secure? Provided for?) She gets a feel of which one treats her best, and who is the best man for the job. High-value women know they are a catch, and they know there are wonderful men interested in women just like them. High-value women are aware that most women settle for whoever they can get, or they are prioritizing the wrong things like a man's looks, sex, or potential. Thus, most women are not actually pursuing the men high-value women are interested in.

Also, a high-value woman is more likely to expand her options when looking for a man who meets her standards. This could mean going to places "outside her comfort zone" where wealthier people gather. It could mean dating a man outside her race, dating a man who is older than her, dating men who are not considered "hot" or "fit" model types. Why? Because she is focused on more than appearance. She is seeking a protective and generous provider. And, she knows that she can *grow* to love any man who is good to her and cares for her.

Love and attraction can blossom when women feel safe, happy, and cared for. Beautiful memories are easily made in secure, peaceful relationships, especially when there is extra money available to play with. All these things are more likely to be present in relationships with high-value men, as opposed to broke, dusty or selfish men. This is something that dusty men and their pickmes do not understand.

My hope is that you were able to resonate with the message of this book, and that you've learned something from even one lesson. This book was written to provide guidance and clarity to any woman who wants to experience more successful and fulfilling relationships with men. Please feel free to revisit this book over and over again. Flip through the pages and or read any of the studies I mentioned in connection to the chapters, anytime that you feel guilty for increasing your standards, expectations and boundaries. Or, whenever you are worried about being too "shallow" towards men. Men use women all the time, and as a result, they get the better end of relationships while women are left with trauma, debt, babies and regret. It is time women learn how to finesse the game in their own favor and gain something positive out of relationships too. May your next relationship (should you choose to engage in one) be happier, safer, and more fulfilling than ever!

Blessing you with pearls of wisdom, always.

Imani Forester

Resources

1. Wolff, H.J. (2017). Marriage Law and Family Organization in Ancient Athens: A Study on the Interrelation of Public and Private Law in the Greek City. Cambridge University Press. Retrieved from https://www.cambridge.org/core/journals/traditio/article/abs/marriage-law-and-family-organization-in-ancient-athens-a-study-on-the-interrelation-of-public-and-private-law-in-the-greek-city/0B1D4021531FE79C17F68A6068681794

2. ILO. (2022, September 18). Closing gender pay gaps is more important than ever. Retrieved from United Nations News website: https://news.un.org/en/story/2022/09/1126901

3. Williams, G. (2013, December 24). More men get alimony from their ex-wives. Reuters. Retrieved from https://www.reuters.com/article/us-divorce-alimony-men-idUSBRE9BN0AW20131224

4. Peterson, R.R. (1989). Women, Work, and Divorce. SUNY Press.

5. Newburger, E. (2019, February 22). A woman's best route to the top 1 percent is to marry rich, research shows. CNBC. Retrieved from https://www.cnbc.com/2019/02/21/a-womans-b

est-route-to-the-top-1-percent-is-to-marry-rich.html

6. Purdue University. (2018, February 13). Money only buys happiness for a certain amount. Retrieved from https://purdue.edu/newsroom/releases/2018/Q1/money-only-buys-happiness-for-a-certain-amount.html

7. International Labour Organization (ILO), Organisation for Economic Co-operation and Development (OECD), & World Bank. (2022, January 9). Female labor force participation. Retrieved from https://genderdata.worldbank.org/data-stories/flfp-data-story/

8. The World Economic Forum. (2020). Global Gender Gap Report 2020. Retrieved from https://www3.weforum.org/docs/WEF_GGGR_2020.pdf

9. Phillip Cohen, "Cohabitation and the Declining Marriage Premium for Men," Work and Occupations 29, no. 3 (2002): 354.

10. Robert F. Schoeni, "Marital Status and Earnings in Developed Countries," Journal of Population Economics 8, no. 4 (November 1995): 357. All as cited in Patrick F. Fagan, Andrew J. Kidd, and Henry Potrykus, "Marriage and Economic Well-Being: The Economy of the Family Rises or Falls with Marriage," (May 2011). Available at http://marri.us/research/research-papers/marriage-and-economic-well-being-the-economy-of-the-family-rises-or-falls-with-marriage/.

11. LeanIn.Org and McKinsey & Company. (2019). Women in the Workplace 2019. Retrieved from https://leanin.org/women-in

-the-workplace/2019

12. V (Fitzpatrick, J.L., Willis, C., Devigili, A., Young, A., Carroll, M., Hunter, H.R., & Brison, D.R. (2020). Chemical signals from eggs facilitate cryptic female choice in humans. Published in the Proceedings of the Royal Society B, 287(1929), 2020 0805. DOI: 10.1098/rspb.2020.0805.)

13. National Center for Education Statistics. (2018-2019). Degrees conferred by race/ethnicity and sex. Fast Facts. Retrieved from https://nces.ed.gov/fastfacts/display.asp?id=72

14. Scharping, N. (2021, June 21). Sexual Cannibalism: Why Females Sometimes Eat Their Mates After Sex. Discover Magazine. Retrieved from https://www.discovermagazine.com/planet-earth/sexual -cannibalism-why-females-sometimes-eat-their-mates-after-sex